The Last Place on Earth

PETER SANSOM was born in 1958 in Nottinghamshire. Now living in Sheffield, he is co-director of the Poetry Business in Huddersfield and editor of *The North* magazine and Smith/Doorstop Books. Carcanet publish his three previous collections, *Everything You've Heard is True*, a Poetry Book Society Recommendation (1990), *January* (1994), for which he received an Arts Council Writer's Bursary and an award from the Society of Authors, and *Point of Sale* (2000), a collection that includes the poetic diary of his year as Marks & Spencer's poet-in-residence. His *Writing Poems* is published by Bloodaxe. He is married to the poet Ann Sansom.

GW00643611

Also by Peter Sansom from Carcanet

Everything You've Heard is True
January
Point of Sale

PETER SANSOM

The Last Place on Earth

CARCANET

Acknowledgements

Many thanks to the editors of the following publications:
Areté, Moving Worlds, My God That's A Huge Colander (ed. the sixth form of St Thomas Aquinas, Birmingham), *The Nottingham Collection* (ed. John Lucas, Five Leaves Press), *PN Review, Poetry Review, The Rialto, Route 57, The SHOp, The Slab* and *Stand*.

'Finest (Half) Hour' was commissioned (thanks Ian!) by Ian Marchant for his book *The Longest Crawl* (Bloomsbury, 2006), and 'The Wife of Bath's Tale' was commissioned by Radio 4, with Elizabeth Spriggs, directed by Jeremy Mortimer.

The fruit poems (thanks Ted!) are for Ted Schofield, and were written as a collaboration with his pencil drawings. They appeared as part of an exhibition in 2005 in Helmsley, North Yorkshire.

I am very grateful for a Royal Literature Fund award in 2002. Grateful thanks too for the support of the Prudential, especially Hannah Breavington and my friends in the Book Club, during which travel several of these poems were started.

First published in Great Britain in 2006 by
Carcanet Press Limited
Alliance House
Cross Street
Manchester M2 7AQ

Copyright © Peter Sansom 2006

A CIP catalogue record for this book is available from the British Library
ISBN 1 85754 885 X
978 1 85754 885 3

The publisher acknowledges financial assistance from Arts Council England

Typeset by XL Publishing Services, Tiverton
Printed and bound in England by SRP Ltd, Exeter

Contents

Crich Stand

A tiny light in all that sea, gone five seconds
and twenty-seven years. One hot July
past chucking-out, we stepped not very drunk
from the Duke of Sussex, six of us, and saw
the landlocked lighthouse. Twenty miles. And set off
there and then to walk all night the White Peak
ups and downs of chevronned lanes; the sky
so very close, so many stars and wishes,
names of constellations over charcoal wheat,
and fingerposts, galleon trees, unseen cattle
lumbering, then a fox that looked through us
and strolled on. In time we stopped, six of us,
somewhere in Derbyshire, where the tower swung
exploding eye-to-eye across the drystone fields.
At seventeen, who needs Dr Freud to say
what it was; and as it is we stood in its wash,
blinded; then turned without a word, our shadows
thrown before us, dreams breaking in
even as we walked, heads down, the half hour
to a bus home. I thought of this today
on what's left of the coast in that neck of the woods,
our old stamping ground, the last place on earth.

and we walked up to school although we knew the school
was closed, a day of sledging on baking trays,
and Spike the Snowman with his dog, Snowy.
The butcher crunched with us the short cut
late and later for work through the little park
and got trapped by his childhood –
rolling the torso, weightlifting the head between us,
and sculpting, setting berries into eyes,
a twig instead of a carrot and bigger twigs for arms.
Our hands burned. All the while the shaken flakes fell
closing the world to the dome of the park
far as the eye and the mind's eye could see.

Ted Savoury

Mr Savoury Duck, who arrived in an ambulance
he converted himself, delivering a music hall
every Tuesday without fail till lumbago
and supermarkets retired him at eighty.
Teabags and tins were no dearer than town, and rabbits
were fanfared alive by the ears, or strung up
for mum to skin with a razor blade for Christmas.
My first football boots really were boots
with the studs nailed in; and his out-of-date
jams and pickles stopped just short of deadly,
though his real talent was getting the world to see
it needed a new mangle or antler coat-stand,
then turning up next week with the very thing.
He stepped out of Dickens before I could read,
with a yard of geese and half a dozen porkers,
and a house up to the rafters in stuffed bears
and cuckoo clocks, unless they were a story
to match the whiskers he grew, a stage-prop,
like the waistcoat and bowtie and cherrywood pipe.
I was eight when he brought the sit-up-and-beg,
huge cast-iron I'd dismount proud at first then
second nature by running it into our hedge,
a feat that from this distance sums up those days
of after the war and before give peace a chance.
And if he earned an honest living by cheating,
everyone knew the rules he didn't play by,
and bought from his van not in spite of but because.

The Day the School Bus Caught Fire

No one was hurt though one or two instead of RE
or physics sat in sick bay nursing shock,
bags and blazers stitched with smoke,
while the road was blocked either end,
firecrew round the blackened shell
like men with a beached whale.

When panic broke loose the kids shouted FIRE!,
which the driver reasonably ignored, till flames
and fumes filled his mirror and stopped the bus,
and the idea spread the fuel tank would go;
then the doors and emergency door opened
and they piled out white-faced and elated

to be counted at a safe distance –
safe: from the room where a parent's world ends.
Safe: the driver free in time to joke at the depot
and the bell telling the kids like any other day
where to be with done or not-done homework,
the felt-tipped hearts of who loves who*m*

and games last thing to dread or look forward to,
in friendship and rivalry closer today
than they will ever be again –
a day that will just pop into their heads
miles from here, decades, today,
the day the school bus caught fire.

Anyone for Tennis?

For its own sake, not for a team or any ambition;
though getting better was everything just then,
at the limit of a junior season ticket
for the gravel courts of Sutton Lawn, with its
leaning pavillion and pissy changing room,
the misspelt graffiti and pulled-out sinks proof.
Mam bought us whites and later matching caps
delighted to find just the thing in Skegness,
and we must have looked prats. Still, our first serves
went in, the topspin backhands put on weight,
and every smash and drop-shot was two fingers
to exams around the corner, that long wet summer.
And when it rained we played on, the meteor
of sopping green splat a passing shot
that left me splay footed, unsighted as I was
by the girl next door flailing for a lob
bra-less in her soaked-through shirt. Advantage us,
me and my best mate, but with no more idea
than chalk dust raised by ace after towering ace
at the All England Club, Wimbledon.

Cross Country

tearing through Bluebell
Wood, the sudden
plank bridge. Slowed
almost to a walk; and
I like that moment,
knowing halfway
I'd lost it,
and going over – felled tree
in PE kit – sploosh
in the fanned wings
of a two-foot stream
the mildest day
of a mild October.
Thirty years.
I can still remember
the struggle and teeter
of giving in.

Poem

It was assembly and *Kes, The Loneliness
of the Long Distance Runner,* a window
onto winding gear at Teversal; and then
it was you
to contradict it with your glamour:

all public school and sixties London, you were
lessons outdoors one day-on-day of summer;
tennis after school and after tennis
the shower I watched you in; you were
the school play you wrote yourself

with me the lead. My writing took your slant,
your Greek e's and buckled y's.
You drove a minibus of us to France
and made *Paradise Lost* hilarious.
You were cynical and believed in us.

Then there was when it was *just* us,
the theatre or golf, jazz or Mozart round at yours,
and the afternoon you let me take the wheel
of your pride and joy
powder blue Volkswagen Beetle.

What you offered those days in good faith
has taken me this far, not far I know but far
for a boy going nowhere, till now
I have the means to write this at least, − at last, −
from wherever I am to wherever you are.

Greenhead Park

The summer after college, the bandstand, the temporary
railings still up somewhere in the seventies,
my canvas shoes torn, a morning dusty
with weeks without rain, papers headlining
with adjectives, hotter-thans. The drunk path
through foisty holly tunnels, the far thonk
of Wimbledon fortnight, all this what is it nostalgia
walks in now with the friend I didn't know then
in a ticket hut, handing out tickets and putters.
Flaubert or Camus and a stroll for a fizzy can
fill his summer and take me out of focus.
July then August, my shorts and cheesecloth,
my hair a generation out of date, a motormower
starting up, and a poster for the open-air Shakespeare
I didn't see year after year, and, similar
and completely different, the whooping shrieks
from the paddling pool so not a part of my life
I never heard them till now.

Breakfast in the Dunblane Hilton

When you were young you said you'd rather die
than live to be old. And yes, perhaps you would rather.
Dorothy Nimmo

I read, surprised by your self, some of your poems –
wise, clear-eyed, cantankerous –, and find
among the Earl Grey, the Frank Cooper's Vintage Oxford,
that I'm crying. Which isn't what your words meant
or even your death. Reading, I'm with you,
not here, this white cloth, electric candelabra,
the Highlands glazed and cut off in frames; until
the big windows green with spring are opened
and the breeze brings a playground's happy chaos
to where we sit. And then, when their bell goes, I remember
just where I am. And close the book, though not
your voice, which stays open – here, like anywhere
you chose to look and listen, and to speak
your mind, your surprised, surprising heart.

To Dorothy Nimmo from Lumb Bank

Across a mile of air a woman talks
right next to us on the hilltop opposite. Acoustics!

Dusk. The moon is a sickle stuck there.

Each year we'd help the same Birmingham sixth form
kick up a storm for a week in words
in March. One day
we walked through the wood to town
and you told me how you started on a course
like this yesterday, years ago. A stick cracked

and a woodpigeon ratcheted away.

In Bookcase I bought *Remains of Elmet*.
'I don't usually accept presents,' you said,
giving me the gift of taking it. *Shh*:

everyone listens as if she were talking
to them. Not dead at all. I mean sometimes
you talk in my head. My brother too.

I could reach out to try the edge, but flinch
from what I know about the moon.
Dorothy,
where are you, when we
need you here.

Ironing

the perfect release of a limited aim
Stanley Cook

I like it best when there's time to see myself
through the drizzle of a weekday morning,
with *Woman's Hour* or a talking-book detective,
and forsythia defining the universe
beyond the propped but empty line. I like
deckchairing the board and plugging in,
the glug of filling the chamber. Then to set off
on the floral reflective cover, a time
that's its own purpose, all faults and craters
levelled to the end of the week. And nothing else
till it's done. Nosing through steam round a button,
powering up the straights of T-shirts,
down the Forth Bridge of a kingsize quilt,
the worst that can happen a cascade of pleats
or a stain to put back soaked in Vanish.
Yes, I've scorched my thumb and melted the nap
from favourite velvet. Yes, that was me, too,
the iron print on the lino. But no,
that was only a joke, the cauliflower ear
of ironing when somebody rings up. And look,
there's the kitten bedded down like an advert in it
with her fleas. The world won't look at me
and say how I've let myself go, the world that loves
to wrinkle and crease and say I told you so.

Finest (Half) Hour

Coming to nothing
from 501 a dozen times a match,
not to mention wall-to-wall practice, over a season
you clock up a fair few miles of seven foot nine and three-quarters,
and yet you seldom see a physique from it. Or you do.
Still, you take it on to live the dream, with the Crucible
next door, spectactular when *for those of you watching in black and white
the pink's behind the blue*. And, sponsored by the same fags,
it flourished for a while in snooker's shadow, an unlikely
spectator sport, three in a bed or needing
five in bits.

I had
Keith Deller's spring-loaded nickel tungstens,
and I shook on the oche, lighting one off another.
Play the board not the man, that's the mantra
till in the end the arrows throw themselves,
a kind of meditation. I'd love to live by it,
but when your middle game's a ton, sixty, forty-five
and he's steady one-forties, it comes home.
And it came home, and it was time
to move on.

It's hard to let go
of hope, though, and there are times even now
I relive that night, that night of nights
the pints paused halfway, when two sets down from nowhere
the one-eighty went in and he went shy at tops
and shy at tops again, and if you can't finish
you're buried, and the whole match turned round.
Leg after leg, if I dropped a dart it went in the sixty,
right to the wire, till in the spotlight
of the team the room the pub holding its breath
I was looking at treble twenty,
treble eighteen,
bull.

Born-again bikers,

top of the range and all the leathers, at their age,
instead of an affair or throwing up the job,
off they go unwinding miles of moonlight road,
travelling in hope, tip-toeing icy bends,

slipstreaming lorries, and wheeling down
the outside of jams, at their age, ducking the Welsh
speed cameras, clocking the gear in Matlock Bath,

and, well, why not, if they see the danger now
they couldn't afford then
and still ride, still open her up,
letting the years fall behind

good luck to them. Haven't I after all
taken up piano.

The bicycle on the other hand

is another world entirely. Always green –
the ozone, depleted stocks, exhaust pipes at buggy height –
and more than that, a style, a way,
the oxygen in your blood, the upbeat start to the day
down a towpath under oak and ash, past playing fields
and the nose-to-tail others I'm one of, watching him go,
with his dayglo helmet and fairtrade back-pack.

I like the idea, a Walkman adding
a soundtrack to even standing on the pedals
up a 1-in-4, like at college – Huddersfield
being like Rome built on seven hills –
because every step put a minute on my life.

Biking it, and wholemeal own-baked, are as near
I suppose as I'll get to living in the Orkneys.
The fountain pen of transport, or vinyl, or milk
on the doorstep for porridge, that's what it is,
not the rainstorm the juggernaut the van that cuts up
the cycle-lane.

How far I've not travelled
since that starting-out years ago, doing the words
for an ad into the small hours,
then locking my push-bike while one of the guys
dropped me home in his Porsche –
next day finding it gone.

Thursday

The sort of morning
I love, grey, on the way
to rain, the drier on,
some music in my head
(The Zombies live in Derby);
down the valley, leisurely
but with effort, a crow
flaps with more for the nest;
a man a mile off
sits astride a roof not waving
with a trowel but working
while the weather holds.
A book, the cat, a pot of tea,
and just for the look of it
a fire in the grate. There is
no reason on God's good earth
why I should
not be happy.

An Easy Riddle
that which shows

Upright freezer like a slow oven.
See-through coffin. What you do
when you've no time, though it
suits me to stand some days
half a morning in this rainforest.
Motor like a ferry crossing,
pre-memory of Mum,
nicely this side of scalding, it's
a pathless dream awake;
downpour of heat from nape
to cleft; virtuous idling,
stepping in in early summer,
stepping out and the world moved on
an entire season.
Where is my life going?

Eight Fruit
Pencil Drawings by Ted Schofield

i   Banana

Like the lad after the war, the Second
World War, who didn't know to peel it,
or like the young woman who missed the double meaning in
'how she cried when she tried my banana'
the banana is always a figure of fun.

Straighten them out for Europe
or open a dockside crate and have the hairy hand
of a six-inch spider walk out, though the real shock's
in how green they are
which in a shop are as yellow as a Cadbury's Flake.

One in each pocket, gunslinger; one down the front,
Tom Jones. It's easy to snigger. Shoot one out
of its skin like spinach from a tin,
swallow it then drop the punchline of
a passerby arse over tip. Humour chock-full of zinc.
Oh Banana! Oh my Fay Wray!

ii   Coconut

Another joke, though more exotic than most
and more useful. Eight feet up a tree in the tropics
with a monkey trained to harvest it, the coconut
got to this page via *Variety*
and the fairground. As I write, the first snow
makes the window an aquarium.
Now I'm at my school, by a huge window,
with the class cast off from the lesson
by just such snow. Then it was
cracked open in the won-coconut, only
to chip at the drift of white and find it was nothing
without chocolate. Coconut my friend,
my old schoolfriend, your healthy head of hair
makes matting and bristles for yard brushes, while the years
split apart, and the window fills with snow

all the time in that classroom and at the Goose Fair
for no reason I know.

iii Grapefruit

Not a melon, and there's only one,
this fruit of B&Bs and American sitcoms,
so it says something that I think of Benny Hill's
high-heeled, low-cut Melanie & co:
which is to say tits, bazookas, breasts, and so
how could I slice this
without meaning a cousin or friend of a friend,
without meaning something serious?

Too late then for a sprinkle of demerara
melting the tart to sweet, a long-handled spoon
easing each juicy and benign segment
to my married, my politically correct mouth.

iv Orange

Looks like it sounds. Except here,
which is grey, except to the mind's eye.
Doubt would kill it. Ash, in two dimensions.
But this *is* orange, and really there's nothing like it –
lemon for instance as a noise just isn't yellow enough;
and you don't even need to look at onion.
(Blackberry, blueberry, redcurrant
only say what they are.) No: orange is on its own.
The zest, when your tongue bursts the peel
of the word, brings the past up close,
close enough to live in now and then:
that duffle coat, those toggles, and a Jaffa
in the breaktime pocket; or the rattle of Halib-
orange, one each tipped bright on your palm
for you and the best friend who called for you.
Or, at the opposite end, the afternoon
you tried Kia-Ora in coffee. And in some scenes
there they are in the days before colour,
Dad, for instance, and Tony and Joss, and Mum
as she was, actually peeling an onion,

like yesterday in the kitchen in the realest
black and white. The chopping board, the thin sharp knife,
no need to see it to see it. I could cry.

v   Peach

The peach is not a political animal.
You can pack it in a crate and load a truck
if you're careful: a peach bursts easily,
and a little consideration pays dividends.
Ship it properly, and warehouse it, wholesale it,
and then at the point of sale
for the sideboard or flan, or even pulped for yoghurt,
then, when all's said and done, you can say
the peach was meant for this. Dumb, and not of course
any sort of animal. The downy flesh
is a metaphor by touch. And what's more,
it's bought and paid for. It's not anything like us.

vi   Pear

This is a singular pear. The stalk a beak,
some grounded bird, just lying there.
Please don't think I'm unaware
if it adopts a posture of despair
or looks maimed or dead,
I know that's just the way I see it.
And maybe, well, *au contraire*
for you it's caught mid-air
in a whirling dance,
a sort of poire-ish Fred Astaire,
the perry that, crushed, makes a cider
to set your hair on end. A fruit
such as the fruit that took Eve
from the garden that was everywhere.

vii   *Pomegranate*

I know the story, I've looked it up,
how half the year, some say a third, the earth
is a wilderness of cold because of it.
And the daughter lost and found, who ate
seven pips from one of these, condemned
as queen of the dead. In here, those self-same
fleshy pips. If you can tell them apart,
take them on your tongue, the field will turn
to the sun, the corpse will sprout
like a seed potato, and new life
will open an eye in your plot of given land –
not this, broken from its little bough
of year-round summer in California.

viii   *Tangerine*

Indistinguishable to the casual eye
or hand or mouth from clementine
confusable with satsuma across a sea
from the factory of a grove, a watermark
hillside, from green to thin and leathery
on the edge of pastel, that blooms
from within, whose peel will give
willingly, the choice that plucks it
from the grasp of its kind.

Sheffield by Night

After the nightclubs have turned out and before
the cleaners have plugged in, the city is as still
as a snowglobe this last day of summer.
I sweat up Paradise St that was Workhouse Rd
and out under green-lit trees of the cathedral
like strolling through an artist's impression;
then over new tramtracks that dad would know
as far as the Cutler's Hall and HSBC.
A dog walking itself in the corner of my eye
past Pollards is gone before I see it's a fox.
Next, Boots the Chemists bright as a cruise ship
but the *Marie Celeste*; then over Fargate
and down Chapel Walk, the Link, the Samaritans,
and double-take at shoes a month's wages;
past the delivery-end of M&S now turn left
by the Crucible. I'm not mugged
in the subway or offered sex to feed a habit.
Ghost roadworks on the steep bit of Flat Street
and in the waking Interchange Paul Simon's
got that ticket still for his destination.
The Grade II listed eyesore on the skyline
is a memory of the Socialist Republic
and in its people-centred daring typical
of Sheaf Field, home of the cyclepath and bendi
-bus, the most wooded city in Europe if you
don't listen to Brum, and the most parks too,
that turned the steelworks into a shopping centre,
and the shopping centre into another world –
then suddenly here, at what I think of as Midland Station,
to carry this lightheaded flu to Nottingham.

On Not Being George W. Bush

The ice-cream carpet, that was one of mine.
And powdered water, wine-gum wine,
jelly windows, see-through cats;
and yo-yo cornflakes, interstellar bobble-hats –
all mine. And mud television and underwater sky,
not to mention the *Who What Why*
Book of Bread. But the river of the recent dead,
that was some other guy.

L.O.V.E.

I live in your heart, biding my time.
Talk with me in a rhyme
or waiting-room paperback.
I bring out the Barry Manilow in you.
The reddest rose appears in your life
and with it the desert pillow.
I am blind, which may be why
I walk you into doors,
metaphorically, literally,
always the last to know.

The Wife of Bath's Tale
as retold by Gladys Ruth Sansom (eighty-six)
of Sutton-in-Ashfield, Notts.

Never had much time for Charlie, but he's all reight to talk to.
Day he come, fost thing he said was he wor fair clammed. Mrs, he
said, me stomach thinks me throat's cut. I said, Well it's bread and
drippin, else you'll have to do like they do in Sheffield. He said,
What's that (never been to Sheffield, only to visit). I said, Do
wi'ert. He laughed and said bread and drippin it is then.

Bread and drippin! As if folks'd give royalty bread and drippin! Our
Joss'd oppened a tin of ham. It wor all done ready in kitchen under
a teatowel. He worn't on his own, the Prince, nayther. We had a
houseload, and it's not a big flat, them as look after him and such,
and them for the telly, and they all wanted snap and a cup of tea.

After he'd had a bite, he said, Well Mrs, you know why we're
here. I said, Aye I do an'all, but it's not me as you want, you want
Clara Do-Rose. He looked at me gone-out, but you're a widder
three times ovver, and my man here said that you know. I said,
That's as may be, but it's Clara Do-Rose as you want. She knows.
She can give you your answer. Well, Clara knows what women
want, and no bogger'd argue with Clara. Mind, I've not seen her
since the war. There was that yank, Doodle Bug we christened
him on account of his tash, but she stuck by her Malcolm, with his
foot blown off, even though he was neither use nor ornament,
never wanted no bogger looking at his foot, even Clara, even in
the dark. Well it don't figure for me, me duck, she told him, but it
were no good, might as well tek a dolly to bed. Even then give her
her due, she never let Doodle Bug do as he liked more than twice
else three times, and she were drunk as a lord one of them as I
know to, because I were wi' her in a car one of them old uns like
you don't see now. It worn't his, we just saw it parked up, and it
were bitter cold and they didn't lock up in them days so he said,
let's gerrin here for a warm. I were in front with, now who wor I
wi'? Clara and Doodle Bug wor in back, hardly got started when
door oppens and it's this Captain whose car it wor.

Anyroad. Next item on the agenda it's Clara hersen, he must have
had her sent for. Never thought to see her in my house. She'd

changed. I said, I'd not know you Clara. And I wouldn't, not with that hair, she had lovely hair. Grow it another couple of inch, you could sit on your hair, that's what her Malcolm said. What would I want to sit on me hair for, she said, me arse'll do me for sitting on. If there's anything wants growing by two inch, Malcolm Dodd, you know where it's billeted. Grow that and I'll sit on it for you. He went bright red, it was in the tap room of the Traveller's, and we were all theer. She didn't care, Clara. I wonder Malcolm didn't land her one, and I think she'd warrant it some nights specially when we'd been out on the qv, but he didn't have the means. Aye, you *do* me lad, you so much as offer, she said, and I'll box your bleedin blindin ears. She had a mouth on her, did Clara, but she had a right hook too. I don't hold with language, not for women anyroad, but she didn't have no choice, he was always so boggering sorry for his-sen, Malcolm.

Anyroad up, the Prince says he'll have another if there's one in the pot and now Clara's here we can get started. Nice manners, but you expect that of royalty. You don't notice his ears so much to his face. But it worn't Clara Do-Rose, not with that hair and her bent double like a safety pin. That worn't the Clara I knew, any bogger could see it worn't her, but I thought if it meks him happy good luck to him, and it did because she says, Yes, she says, I can tell you, and I'm the only one as can.

The prince said, 'You can?' Room went quiet: well, it matters, this, to him. Because his mam's had this message from God in the middle of doing a jigsaw of their house, about handing on the reins or throwing the towel in for good. She said God had said, Let Charles tek ovver now lass, only you've got to set him a test fost. She says What's that then God? He says, There's more women in your country than men, and it's not reight as things stand, women should have more say. So for a start your lad Charles has to tell you what it is that women want. And this answer, what women want, it's got to be an answer that not one woman in the country'd disagree wi'. Either he tells you that or he don't get the kingdom, no bogger does, because it's going to be one of them like France or America where they don't have no royalty. Tell him he's got a year and a day, God says. Then he thinks again and says, Nay, with all this helicopters and satellites and such tell him he's got a week.

So Charles, he goes rushin round like a blue-arsed fly. Asking everybogger. Archbishop of Canterbury, Chief of Police, Lionel

Blair. Then he has a brainwave and asks his dad, what he thinks it is his mum wants. Apparently Philip says, I don't know as she wants owt, lad, she's not short of a bob or two. But he's been tipped the wink that Charles has to ask a widder three times ovver living round our way. In a council flat. Course that's me, and here we are. But it worn't me.

And Clara Do-Rose, or her as says she's Clara Do-Rose, says again, Yes, and I'm the only bogger on God's earth as *can* tell you. And it wor reight quiet, as I say, apart from the chuntering of them cameras. Then she says, I'll tell you summat for nowt, though, that sort of information don't come cheap. Now Clara's Malcolm wor like that, so mean he wouldn't let you light a candle off his lamp; but not Clara. She were always oppenhanded. We'd say, Clara you'll never have no money so long as you've a hole in your arse. And bonny, she wor proper bonny, and now I think on she wor a lot like that wife of his what killed hersen or ran off with a foreigner, I know it wor summat o' sort. Car crash that wor it, I think. I do know they took snooker off. Nowt on telly, Joss said, that Princess Dinah's died. Aye, it wor a long day that one.

But this Clara Do-Rose, when she said that about it not coming cheap, well she looked just like one of them what-do-you-call-its. I'm not joking. Manny and mardarse at same time. Charlie says, Mrs, you can name your price.

Door went just then. It wor our Joss, he'd been out for more milk. They'd only got sterra, he says, and, By, it's a top coat warmer out theer. And he stops, cos cameras's going. But this is what they want, the news men. Cameras going and it's all lit up for the telly. I'll mash some tea, he says, and he goes.

She says, I don't want no money. There's this pause. And she says, I want him. And she points at this young feller as is with the prince. Not long out of school, by the looks on it. Not married, are you me duck? she says and he laughs but she's not laughing.

Sorry Mrs, the prince says, Sir Dooins is not for sale, ask for anything, what do you want: wealth, jewellery, a palace...

She says, I've always fancied owning a racehorse. And Charlie's face lights up. But no, she says, only Sir Dooins here will do, his hand in marriage. She grins her one-tooth at him, and gives him this wink. Charlie tells the telly men to turn their tackle off and bogger off out onto the landing.

When they've gone, Sir Dooins says, Mrs, I will marry you whenever you wish. Charlie says you'll do no such thing Gerald or Jason or whatever his name is. And this lad says, But Your Highness, it's not for my country, I'm doing it for you. I thought he wor going to cry, the prince, he wor that moved. You can hear the clock going now, too big for the room. Charlie sits reight still for a bit like he's thinking reight hard, says summat quiet to the lad, who nods, and then says summat else quiet to the man with the briefcase, and this man says, We'll have one of them contracts drawn up.

Nay, says Clara, we don't need no contracts. If you agree here and now to wed me, no lawyer'll wangle you out on it, not in this world. What do you say? And the lad, this Sir Dooins, says alright and they shake hands, I do this for the Prince. Clara says (and you've got to remember she's seventy, nay she'll be eighty-odd), she says, Give ovver, it's nowt to do with him, you can't help yoursen can you? Men, you're all the same, led ovver the fields by your willy-nilly.

Not fields though, now, it's all built up round that way. Tek the precinct. I remember when it was Idlewells, though I lived out at Bleak Hall in them days, Tod's Row it wor called then. Oh yes, tell you who I went to school wi' as you'll know: Harold Larwood. Pub named for him now up Annesley. It'd surprise if me dad isn't in there this minute, though I can't tell you the last time he called round here. It's a few years. A good few years since I've seen me dad. I don't know where he is these days tell the truth. He said, Don't you worry, you can take your hat off, Fanny Ann, I can see you've had your hair cut. He never wanted me to have me hair cut, didn't me dad. Finest fast bowler England ever had and he might just as well have not bothered if you ask anybogger. Harold Larwood. Harold Larwood, George Formby, you don't hear nowt on them nowadays, Dr Steiney, you never see him nayther. Nor our Tony.

So they call back the telly men and set the cameras going for what all women want. Even with all that you can still hear the clock ticking and everybogger holding their breath. Well? the prince says. Hold your hosses, Clara says, you've got to stand up and ask me reight. So the Prince of Wales stands up in my living room and says, Mrs Do-Rose, Tell us now what it is that all women want. And she smiles. You'll notice my fiancé there, he's got lovely big hands, she says, and it's true what they say I can tell you, she says, and that's one of the reasons I decided he wor for me. Women don't want a man for decoration.

But nay, I'm only teasing, that's not it, or not all there is to it, not by a long chalk. Anyroad she says, What women want, it's what you'd expect. And she pauses like. Then: women want to be in charge of their-sens. After a moment Charlie nods, Ay, he says, to be their own boss, like, happen you're right. Me mam'll agree with that I should think. And well, as you know, she does agree an all, and we're into all this parliament rigmarole.

But then it's not a week later, and it's the wedding isn't it in London. I don't go, not with this leg, but I see it on telly like everybogger else. Well Clara's a sight. Old enough to be his grandma and falling down drunk even at the altar, and when it comes to her vows she says, I f—in well do, and laughs so you can see she's not reight in head.

All ovver bar the shoutin, I think, when who should come round next day but Charles again, and on his own an all.

Well, we've got nowt in house and it's days since Joss went round with the Ewbank, but he says he's not stoppin. So Joss mashes a pot of tea and finds out a packet of fig biscuits and half a layer of teatime assorted. The prince has brought some photos of the happy couple (that's what he called them). Seems as Clara made him bring them for old time's sake. And in the photos it really is Clara Do-Rose. I mean the Clara as was. Beautiful. I couldn't believe it. Charlie pours another cup and tells me how it's come about, which is this: After the wedding, they went somewhere posh for the reception, and after somewhere grand for the wedding night. Well this Sir Dooins, he's a perfect gentleman and even though she's nasty, I mean not just to look at, I mean nasty in hersen, mardy and allus on, like one of them little dogs that pees up your sofa because it can't sink its teeth in your leg. Nevermind that, he's lovely with her all the same. But that's him, Charles says, that's him, generous in his heart, like one of the old-fashioned knights, the knights of the round table, I forget which one he said. It worn't Albert I do know.

And on his wedding night, just as it's dropping dark, he's looking out across at the gardens to the river reight far off, just stood theer, Sir Dooins, at his winder, a bit worried obviously. In comes his bride. He hears but don't turn round at fost. But it's Clara like in the photo, the beautiful Clara Do-Rose, nineteen else twenty. Clara Do-Rose at nineteen. She could pass for nineteen till she wor thirty, as a matter of fact, them nights we went singing down the Market Tavern and the Soldiers and Sailors, the Traveller's Rest, the Dog and Duck, the Staff of Life, touring round. When a song come on the wireless we liked we'd write it down on a sugar bag and practise in front room and go out of a night and sing for us larrup till chucking-out time, pissed up, Malcolm never objected nor mine. So this is Clara as she wor when I knew her. When he turns to her, Sir Dooins can't believe his eyes. This isn't the woman he wed. Ah but it is, she says, I'm Clara Do-Rose reight enough.

And this is it: because you loved me, because you saw into who I wor, this is who I am tonight on our wedding night. Well they hug each other, like they would. Then she steps back. But, she says, you've got to choose. I can be like this, and young as I am now, for only half the time. At night or else in the day. Before or after sunset I have to be the old Clara Do-Rose again. Which is it to be, my husband, she says, old by day or in your bed?

(Joss worn't taking it in at all; he said, They're closing that Kwiksave. Are they really, his Highness says. He's alright, he'll just go down the precinct like he used to. They've finished the precinct, done it up, put a roof on it, made a nice job on it an all.)

Anyroad where wor I? Yes. So Sir Dooins has to choose, day or night. She says, Clara does, You've got till tomorrer to mek your mind up. Quick as a flash, he says, I don't need till tomorrer me duck. I know what my answer is. Clara interrupts, Ayup lad be careful now, I know you men, thrice nightly fost week and it's off down the allotment theerafter – don't you be hasty. Sir Dooins raises his hand. Nay, Mrs, he says, I said I know what my answer is and I'm sticking to it: young by day or young by night, that's for *you* to decide.

Now the prince gets excited telling this and the bottom half of his bourbon's come away in his tea. This is the best part he says, it's like a fairy story, he says because Clara Do-Rose when she hears

35

him say that she's reight glad because now she can be young all the time, and she is. You see, it's like brokken a spell, him saying as it's up to her, seeing as she's her own boss.

I say, So they live happily ever after then do they? Looks like it, he says. And what about you, your highness, I say, you get to be king now do you? He sets off on it but I stop him, I don't need to know all the ins and outs o' Meg's arse. There's the door and it'll be our Maureen and Diane or our Maureen and Mick. But it's me dad. Oh dad, I've fair missed you, I say, I can't think of owt else. And he sits there, large as life, still wi' his boots on. You'll never guess, he says, who I've just been talking wi'. But I know, I don't know how: Harold Larwood, I say, and it wor an all, took the wind out on his sails. But ayup father, can you see we've got company? Dad, this is the Prince of Wales. Your Highness, this is me dad. And I didn't know where to put mesen because me dad just said, I can see that, and what's it to me: I only died for such as him. And happen he did because the prince said, Mester, I know as you did, I do know that very well. And they shake hands. By it wor a sight, as if they wor the same man underneath. Well they wor, and that's a thought, your dad and your king as will be, your dad and your king the same man, it struck me of a sudden. And both on 'em beholden, beholden to me or my kind, and me and my kind beholden to them an all, or to him and his kind, if you follow me, that's how it is. Living or dead, woman or man, then or nar.

The Brotherton Library, University of Leeds

I walk along the gallery in the rotunda, back again though at first I
don't know it beside the *Romantics in their Letters,* a private joke at
my own expense. It goes on as it always does, while below, at
leather desks, lamps reveal a dozen dead minds open at the spine.
Then I go down to sit at a desk too. And start a new plot of words.
My family, it seems to be, the one I grew up with, dead themselves
most of them, but almost more likely to walk in today than ever in
their lives. I like the idea that they might meet themselves coming
round again, or I like how it sounds, that they might meet themselves in me.

Living Room

Carpet we stick to, flowers underfoot;
a velour suite in water moss, brand new
to us in a borrowed van from Stoke;
a shouting telly; low nicotine ceiling,
nets at the window; condensation.
The cloth stays on, polythene, pooled
in folds with tea, sugar grains, and grease
where once was next to godliness.

A walking frame; lifeboat
calendar two years out of date;
and pride of place to family
in pubs, on holiday, cutting a cake
on the mahogany-coloured unit:
one cupboard a dispensary,
the other a distillery.

On the Road

I'd like to be a lorry driver, sometimes,
if it weren't for reversing, manoeuvring
in towns, if it weren't for unloading
and customs. My reward
the greasy joes, a jukebox like Brian Matthews,
a game of pool, and a calendar of girls
in the cab, their smile in October and November
the most they wear. I'd like sometimes
to drive a lorry A-known to B-known
and the route between to a deadline
with a stop-over in a lay-by and the kettle
plugged in the cigar lighter.
And to smoke again incidentally
Player's No. 6 like everybody,
nearside lane a steady 65,
wipers this year next year this,
the continent an adventure,
the moon over pine forest, if it weren't
for the ring-road, the tachometer,
if it weren't for the belly
and the beard our Johnno shaved off
they said (it was a talking point) before
he hanged himself that morning
in a warehouse outside Crewe,
despite a wife, waiting,
despite a child.

Joss

I'm asleep when I see him these days. Two men
lift him in a wheelchair outside the house:
the wind or some force turns the airborne wheels.
That sleeveless jumper, collar and Labour Club tie,
dark round the jowls though just wet-shaved, it's him,
Ray Reardon hair and smile, the waxworks gazing
wherever they point him, jostled, into a van.

There's a full moon in the corridor. I put on
the glasses I don't yet need to read
the flowering seas, a couple of which he's named,
who in this life couldn't read, no one ever
having taught him or taught him he could learn.
I don't remember anyone hugging him,
no one ever I think even held his hand,
even at the end. Pneumonia, the old man's friend.
He was my brother and my friend. And not old
or not to me. Now I go back to see him,
he closes his book no wiser and no less wise.

We All Dance In Our Family

i.m. Cynthia Greensmith

'We all dance in our family,' you said, keeping your patience
as the record ended. 'You just go with it.'
The Dansette clunked another 45 and Elvis crackled out.
I was eight or nine, old enough you thought to learn to dance.
You learned I'd two left feet. And so – glamorous,
the front room a dance hall – you danced with your daughters.

Twenty years later, you danced again in Mum's front room,
though by then it was a flat. My wedding reception.
The family pulled out all the stops. We love a do – a fuddle –
any excuse, a birthday Agadoo or Anniversary Waltz.

That day you'd danced already, in the kitchen –
baking was dancing too, a way to celebrate, to love:
a practical, generous dance; and much the same as
when you took the bride and groom aside –
knowing your own mind and how the world worked –
to tell us the secret of a happy marriage.
You were right too, having been married to Dave forever.

Meanwhile, they were up to roll out the barrel. Everybody,
and our Tony in among, glazed with sweat, the life and soul,
we're going to do the Twist, and it goes like this.

And when the party ended, we joined in Maureen's heartfelt
I had a little drink about an hour ago...
Even going home was a dance. I think the world
was a dance for for you, Cynth, a way
of going with it, of living in the moment,
of living the most of life.

I

To look at me
I'm a one or ell,
a stick, a stand, an upright,
that door seen from the side,
the rope into an imagined well.

But if you'll just listen
I could see. Fanciful, a camel
might pass through me, gold thread,
or more likely instead
I'll sprout in a sack of potatoes.
Then again, drop the aitch
and up I goes,
lofty or on something. But what I

really am these days,
the mirror of my punning says,
is my dad, except
he was more flat cap than smart alec,
and I'd be Clear As Mud.
Too daft to laugh at?
I, lad. I.

Snow. I's down.
Horizontal,
the short line's called
that underlines us all.
But never grave. And Y?
He did not take I seriously.

Which is fine, until
he never said what he meant.
Nor me. Until he's
the hyphen between dates,
and I's
too late.

Dying

Not me. Or so slowly I don't notice.
This is just visiting, staring at subsidised tea
from the very same volunteer
as twenty years ago and sixty miles away,
when the first of us began to disappear.

Other times I followed a line on the floor
like a fairytale or myth to be pictured
as bone, like a grave or puppetry,
until, tibia and fibia, spinal column and skull
I could take up my skin and walk free.

These grown-up years I've dropped in often
on wards long and intimate as a beach,
gossip bouncing two and three beds down,
or dozed with them bound to a monitor and drips
on nights they'd not last till dawn

but found them wheeled out next day
wide awake and waving like royalty.
Reprieve, reprieve. And it's true, broken can be made
better than new: this can be stopped in its tracks,
that can at least be delayed.

But not always, and not forever,
which is why we're all here. For a while
she knows me, and her hand grips mine.
But then again she wants her mum.
And who can blame her? It's time.

Bluebell Wood

We're no gardeners, me even less so,
going at our bindweed and stinging nettle,
the egg yolk suns of dandelions; till here,
in May, the lovely violet blush
of bluebells no one planted. Bluebells
to bring back in their gouache mist
me and the dog, running, clodded furrows
giving way to Dumble Wood, and then the track

like a funnel into Bluebell Wood, in that
proud Harriers' vest, where we'd turn
in a curve for home through the lilac dusk
of harebell, wild hyacinth, wood hyacinth,
the furthest I'd been alone, me and the dog,
out to an Arctic Circle or Timbuctoo
that everybody knew: 'You've been up Bluebell Wood?'

Then one year it was gone, just like that,
for a link road ten minutes quicker
to Mum's, to Tony's, to see Mick or Donald,
all of them, Auntie Olive, our Cynth, our Joss.
Bluebell Wood, right here, across the decades
of our garden, packed tight, and in among
is Dad, though he knew better, singing that
Bluebells are bluebells are blue bells are blue.

Autumn

To be out in stillness after days of gales
and pitch the rake into drifts of leaves –
it feels good, like jogging, but useful too
and, on the shared steps under the ash,
neighbourly. I might do some of the street.
A third bin bag filled by ten, and a fourth,
for the tip. Better would be to pile them up
and while I'm at it drag a fallen branch,
maybe lop the Russian Vine and wind it on;
then a slosh of petrol from the can we've not got
out of the shed (ditto), and to set light to it all.
And for the family to stand, a tableau
round the Brueghel reds and golds, eyes stinging
in the wholesome smoke. A job well done. Except,
after the attics went and what nearly happened,
we don't do fire, only tamed in the grate, and sometimes
what we think we hear, or smell, or wake from.

'I'd heard about the man who, drunk'

I'd heard about the man who, drunk, stood up
and said, This is where I get off, then opened
a moving door and jumped. A friend
of a friend pulled the communication cord.
It came to mind and I told the story, and then
this person remembered standing next
to a boy who lowered the window,
and stuck out his head. Decapitated,
was all she said. But I saw a guillotine
and the torso turning back, going on
like they say a chicken does, and this person
stepping aside to let the boy go
wherever it was he last thought he should go.
And so when this person said Are you really
married, it was easy to say Oh yes.

July Football at Abbeyfield Park

What was me and Tom playing three-and-in's
become twenty-odd of us, toddlers to grown men
up and down the twilight in slip-on (off) shoes,
or Beckham 7 shirts and Nike boots, oblivious
to the swifts and/or bats and the brilliant armada
of hot air balloons over Attercliffe.
The swings at the far end are deserted now
of teenagers with their cans; a dog-walker
shouts to a bush; and at once the crown green's
empty, most of them in the Tollgate
where Roy will be thinking of calling time.
At the offy too Shaheena's slotting the grilles
onto the windows, though she'll stay open
till they turn out, which means we can stop
on our way back, clarted up and dripping with sweat,
for milk and bread and nearly yesterday's paper.

Late Afternoon Wedding, Christchurch, Pitsmoor

The recorded tongues of bells, Saturday,
down our chimney, point only one way
while I lay sticks and balance the coal

at the corner of Nottingham Road
and Pilgrim Street, where it's dark with trees,
branches broken this time of year, and I picture
a conga of cars down to the bottle-bank
and up to the Working Men's. I like it,
the Vicar of Dibley coming out to really laugh
among the saying-cheese, turning a blind eye
to confetti: it's life all right, dove grey top hats
on dreadlocks and one February the bride's
acres of lace set off by fingerless white gloves
and milk-white Doc Martens. The firelighters

light the only time I read the paper (Iraq,
a footballer) while the vicar's called to her next,
tracked by a cousin with a camcorder. The evenings
are coming on and in my mind's eye the girl
starting her shift early has changed her pitch
as she does from discretion or simply
better business a hundred yards down Pye Bank;

and, though the sticks have taken enough to spit,
I stay on the hearth, reliving my childhood
with the silverfish and a happy leap of flames
till the bells, like traffic or a clock, return
louder than ever by stopping mid-peal.

BE 243 18:20 Belfast to Bristol

I sit in mid-air over mountains of cloud
and the fingerprinted sea in among,
knowing the slightest thing about flying.
And when I bail out, as I often do, the chute
catches on a strut and makes me climb the straps
to free me at these hundreds of miles an hour
and let my mind let go. It's a failure
of imagination not to be terrified.

At twenty I crouched in pumps up the slates
to turn an aerial. At thirty I froze at the top
of the ladder, astonished that, older,
my body knew better. Like the time,
hitchhiking, I stepped from the guy's car
at journey's end, having calmly declined,
only to find I was shaking to pieces.

The Isle of Man is a relief map. Three little spurts
of boats aim for the same harbour. It's pressure
keeps us up here and lets us breathe.

Coming down is a bronco in a thunderstorm. Thrown about,
nobody seems to mind, least of all me, here:
in this gripping thriller or genius poem,
this summer of childhood, what prayer must be
if you can do it, and what love sometimes is,
as we know, me and you,
or our bodies do.

The Day He Met His Wife

She said goodbye to common sense
and so they booked a room
in an afternoon hotel to holiday
with fecklessness in laundered sheets;
and there was an orchid
and a crisp new paperback,
the art gallery on a working day,
a second bottle opened and a third
knowing tomorrow in twenty years
they'd wake with such a head,
a sink full of pots, the fridge
empty as Antarctica
and everything uphill again
in rain you could canoe
the middle of the street down,
which they did.